DOUGLAS MELINI

MILES
McENERY
GALLERY

525 West 22nd Street   511 West 22nd Street   520 West 21st Street
New York NY 10011   New York, NY 10011   New York NY 10011

DOUGLAS MELINI: HERE AND NOW

By Sara Roffino

A subtle chain of countless rings
The next unto the farthest brings;
The eye reads omens where it goes,
And speaks all languages the rose;
And, striving to be man, the worm
Mounts through all the spires of form.

—Ralph Waldo Emerson

All conscious beings on this planet will remember exactly where they were and what they did over the past year and a half. We will recall the paths we walked, the sounds we heard, the tastes and smells seeping into and forever altering our psychological and physical compositions. There will be a certain nostalgia. Shared trauma creates bonds. As we all Zoomed in, we also zoomed out. Screens but also hikes. Spores on the lettuce alongside blockchain technology and decentralized economies. Such simultaneous expansion inward and outward has a certain logic. The telescope and the microscope were both invented around the turn of the 17th century, within twenty years of each other. Near, far. In, out. Object or image. Or both, meeting right here, right now.

Ceci n'est pas une pipe. This is a tree. And a painting.

As these past months have warped time and space, simultaneously stretching them out and forcing them to contract, social norms have dissolved, and conventions at large have became null. Throughout the COVID-19 pandemic, Douglas Melini worked at home and in his Jersey City studio, creating two bodies of work that both mirror and embody the larger shifts that have rippled through our lives. The culmination of his inquiries is *Intelligent Life Forms*, an exhibition of paintings and collages that dissolves art historical conventions, proving one need not subscribe to dogmas that require unilateral cohesion to Concept or Form, Romance or Reason. His presentation is both a rigorous examination of material and color, and an ethereal homage to nature. In sum, it is a call to observe the forces, seen and unseen, that shape our existences from the cellular level through to the spiritual.

As Melini tells it, an almost ecstatic experience deep in the Oregonian forest was the beginning of these two bodies of work. While hiking alone several years ago, he was suddenly faced with the presence of his own childhood self. The event triggered a visceral awareness of the interconnectedness of the universe and species, something akin to an awakening or transcendence. Such openings have been a part of human experience since the beginning of time—often, but far from always, brought about by the ritual consumption of psychoactive plants and fungi. The ancient Greeks first conceived of the Great Chain of Being, an idea that has shaped religious, cultural, and political thinking since it was proposed more than two millennia ago. For Aristotle, Plato, and later Plotinus, the universe existed according to a metaphysical hierarchy in which God was at the top, and all other beings and matter filed into strata below, deeply interconnected and interdependent. The Great Chain of Being was the foundation of Neoplatonic thinking, which understood all experience and existence as one. The idea later germinated in monotheistic religions as well as within scientific inquiry, preceding Carl Linnaeus's *Systema Naturae* (1735), the taxonomy still used to categorize species; and Charles Darwin's *On the Origin of Species* (1859), which introduced his theory of evolution.

Twenty years before Darwin published *On the Origin of the Species*, the American transcendentalists adapted the Great Chain of Being for their own needs: less God, more divinity as nature. Ralph Waldo Emerson introduced the original version of his 1836 essay "Nature" with an epigraph from Plotinus. When he republished the text in 1849, his own words (reprinted at the beginning of this essay) opened the text.

Emerson's worm is Melini's mushroom. The subterranean mycelium networks stretch for miles, serving as information superhighways for plants and trees, enabling them to communicate with each other, share nutrients, and fight off invasive species. Above the earth, mushrooms are the beginning and end of all life forms, helping to break down dead matter and feed it back into the ground to stimulate new growth. They also have the capacity to help heal trauma and reshape the physiological elements of the brain and therefore sentience itself. Culled from field guides used by mycology hobbyists to determine which fungi are safe to eat and which are fatal, the highly stylized mushrooms in Melini's collages become almost individual subjects, anthropomorphized characters in a drama. From a distance, Melini's watercolor works on paper appear as richly hued, dense abstractions. But upon a closer encounter with the works, the hundreds of different mushroom shapes, colors and sizes emerge, dancing around the perimeter of the paper and serving in some sense as a frame for the color studies within. Melini uses no brushes in his application of the watercolor paints that constitute the interior of the collages, allowing the pigments to coalescence into a deep space, creating a simple differentiation between foreground and background. Though smaller in scale and subtler in presence, Melini's mushroom collages are the foundation upon which his paintings are conceived and made.

While designing and sourcing the frames for the mushroom collages, Melini realized that distressed wood (usually poplar, maple, or pine sourced from dismantled 18th-century barns) offered a depth of material as well as a conceptual complexity in terms of its relationship to the mushroom and to the history of painting. He began using wider planks of the wood to build components for his paintings. Saturating them with color through a rigorous staining process, the planks are placed to form L-shapes, with each work containing two sets of Ls in two contrasting colors. The palettes are aggressive, like the "sweet and sour" description once applied to Peter Halley's canvases.[1] The two Ls are placed exterior to a heavily built-up canvas, and interior to the finish frame. Melini's doubling up of "frames" dislodges the notion of a fixed interior and exterior. The eye is drawn *into* the planks of wood, tracing the natural deep furrows and ridges of the material. The central canvases, meanwhile, are built up and out with meaty paint, to the point that the center shape of each work becomes an almost sculptural protrusion outward into space. The effect is a subtle, but persistent, optical vibration. Melini's finish frames match the colors of the interior canvas. This at first seems to neatly package the oneness of the painting as a discrete object, but in fact it emphasizes a false belief that some elements of the work are moving inward and others are moving outward.

6

A cursory viewing of Melini's work could box it in as pure formalism, but Melini was trained at the California Institute of the Arts, or CalArts, a sure indicator that there is more going on than meets the eye. Melini's use of wood in these paintings stirs a connection to the Belgian surrealist René Magritte. And once Magritte enters the equation, it's impossible not to see Melini's paintings as a response to or continuation of the inquiries posed by *The Treachery of Images*, painted by Magritte in 1929. Despite its rather diminutive size, *The Treachery of Images* (is it a pipe or a painting of a pipe?) influenced the conceptual giants Marcel Broodthaers and Marcel Duchamp, and instigated discussions that dominated European and North American art in the twentieth century—about representation, readymades, assemblage, and the very nature of what does and does not constitute art. A tree may not be art when it is in the forest, but removed from its natural habitat and saturated with color it can become a piece of art.

1. Jeff Gibson, "Peter Halley," *Artforum*, December 2017.

René Magritte, *The Treachery of Images (This is Not a Pipe) (La trahison des images [Ceci n'est pas une pipe])*, 1929, oil on canvas, 23 ¾ x 31 ¹⁵/₁₆ x 1 inches, 60.33 x 81.12 x 2.54 cm Los Angeles County Museum of Art. Purchased with funds provided by the Mr. and Mrs. William Preston Harrison Collection (78.7) © 2021 C. Herscovici / Artists Rights Society (ARS), New York

Melini's paintings are the formal descendants of Josef Albers, Sol LeWitt, and Frank Stella. Spiritually, their most direct forbear is Ad Reinhardt, whose drive to create paintings that invite contemplation was influenced in part by his close decades-long friendship with the Trappist monk Thomas Merton. Preceding them all, of course, was Wassily Kandinsky. The father of abstraction introduced the German idea of "Stimmung" early in his seminal 1910 text *Concerning the Spiritual in Art*, describing it as an "inner feeling" that can be expressed through art. It is "food for the spirit," he writes, "where the observer becomes conscious of a responsive vibration within his soul."

If the trees, the mushrooms, and their co-dependency are the facts of this show, color is the language through which they are expressed. Emerson writes that "nature always wears the color of the spirit." Melini's landscapes can perhaps be thought of as color studies of the spirit, both his own and those of all that exist within the Great Chain of Being. ∎

Sara Roffino is writer and editor based in Brooklyn, NY. She is currently an Artseen editor for *The Brooklyn Rail*.

Untitled (Tree Painting-Double L, 3 Greens), 2021
Oil on linen and acrylic stain on reclaimed wood with artist frame
63 ¼ x 71 ¼ inches
160.7 x 181 cm

Untitled (Tree Painting-Double L, Yellow, Orange, and Light Blue), 2021
Oil on linen and acrylic stain on reclaimed wood with artist frame
52 ¼ x 52 ¼ inches
132.7 x 132.7 cm

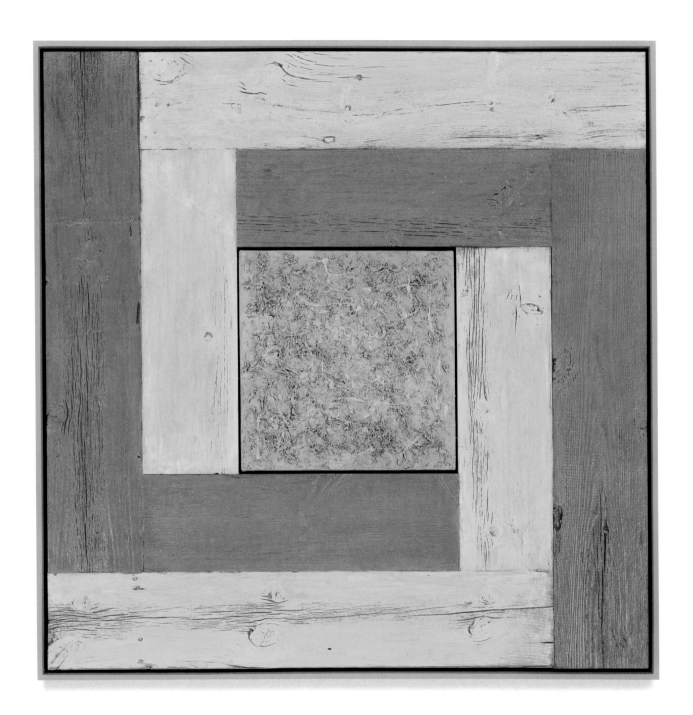

Untitled (Tree Painting-Double L, Magenta, Purple, and Lavender), 2021
Oil on linen and acrylic stain on reclaimed wood with artist frame
54 3/8 x 54 3/8 inches
138.1 x 138.1 cm

Untitled (Tree Painting-Double L, Black, Blue and Red), 2021
Oil on linen and acrylic stain on reclaimed wood with artist frame
52 ³⁄₈ x 52 ³⁄₈ inches
133 x 133 cm

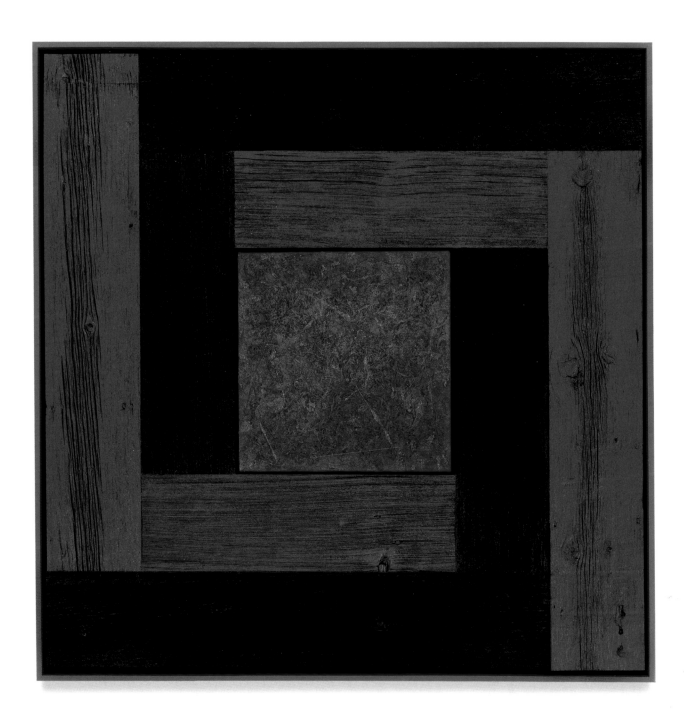

Untitled (Tree Painting-Double L, Blue, Pink, and Yellow), 2021
Oil on linen and acrylic stain on reclaimed wood with artist frame
52 ¼ x 52 ⅛ inches
132.7 x 132.4 cm

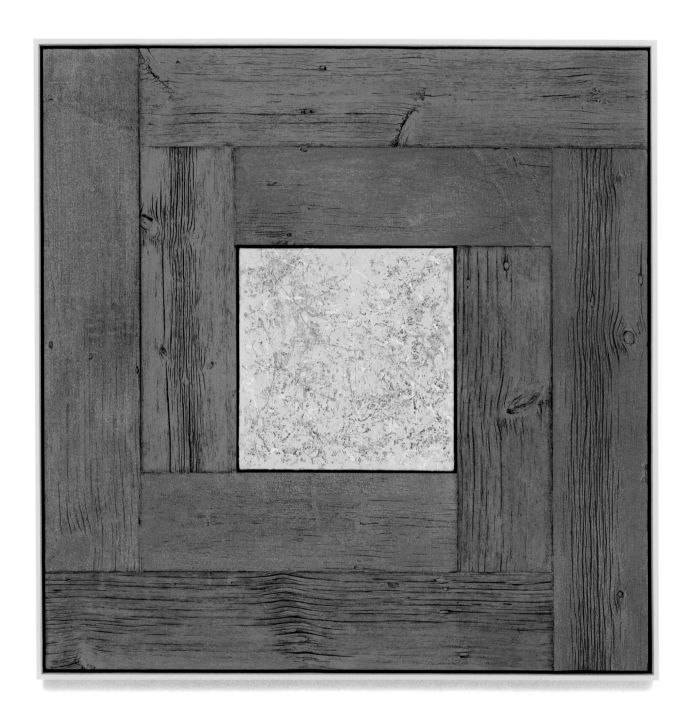

Untitled (Tree Painting-Double L, Blue, Green, and Black), 2021
Oil on linen and acrylic stain on reclaimed wood with artist frame
52 ³/₈ x 52 ³/₈ inches
133 x 133 cm

Untitled (Tree Painting-Double L, Red, Blue, and Green), 2020
Oil on linen and acrylic stain on reclaimed wood with artist frame
33 ⅞ x 33 ⅞ inches
86 x 86 cm

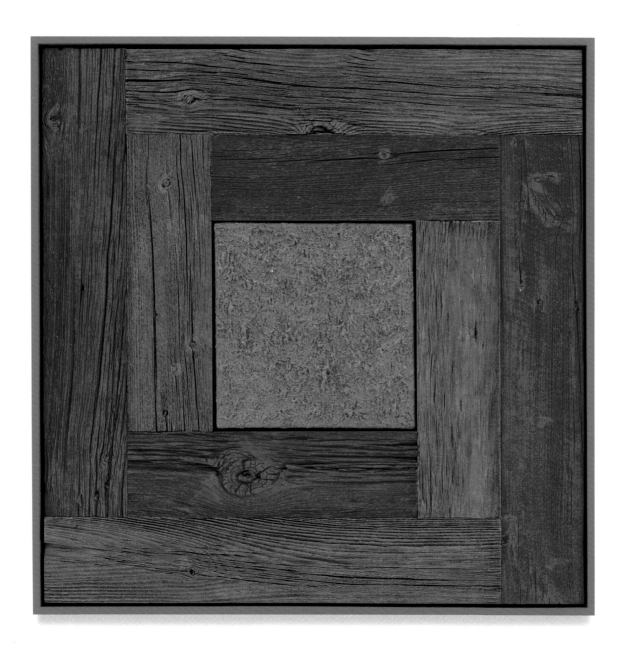

Untitled (Tree Painting-Double L, Yellow and Gray), 2021
Oil on linen and acrylic stain on reclaimed wood with artist frame
52 ¼ x 52 ⅜ inches
132.7 x 133 cm

Untitled (Tree Painting-Double L, Pink, Orange, and Blue), 2021
Oil on linen and acrylic stain on reclaimed wood with artist frame
62 7/8 x 71 inches
159.7 x 180.3 cm

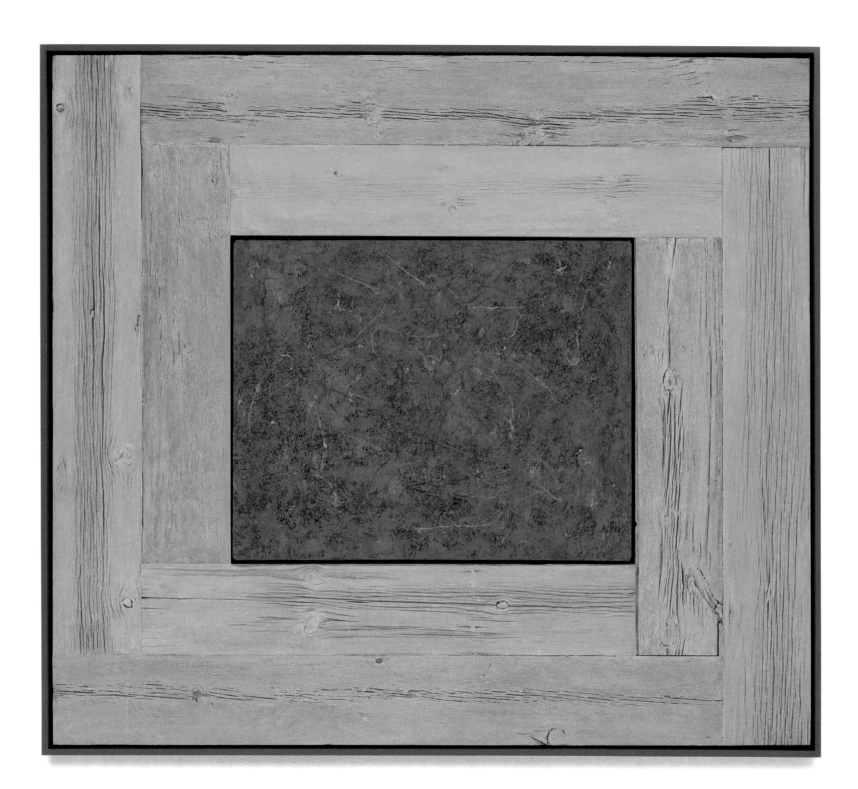

Untitled (Tree Painting-Double L, Pink and Black), 2020
Oil on linen and acrylic stain on reclaimed wood with artist frame
51 ¼ x 51 ¼ inches
130.2 x 130.2 cm

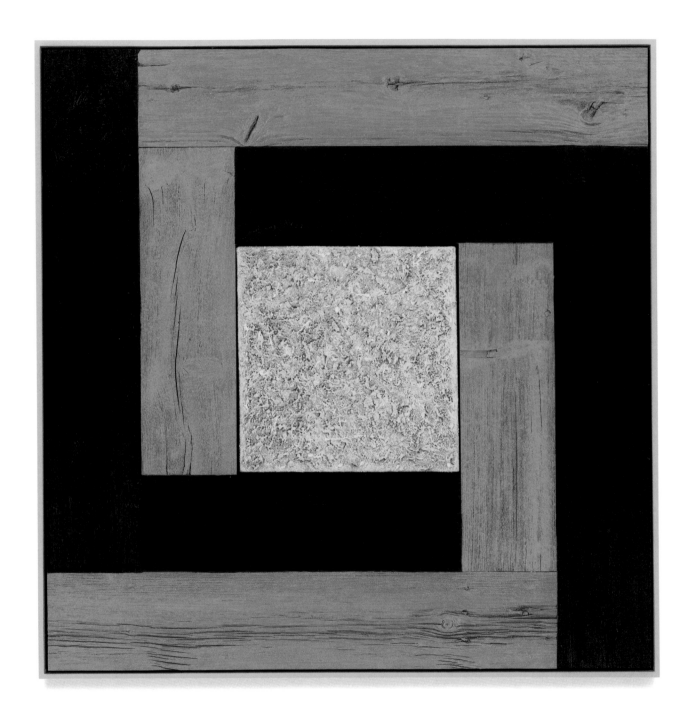

Untitled (Tree Painting, Full Spectrum/Purple), 2019
Oil on linen and acrylic stain on reclaimed wood with artist frame
42 x 42 inches
106.7 x 106.7 cm

Untitled (Tree Painting, Full Spectrum/Yellow), 2019
Oil on linen and acrylic stain on reclaimed wood with artist frame
42 x 42 inches
106.7 x 106.7 cm

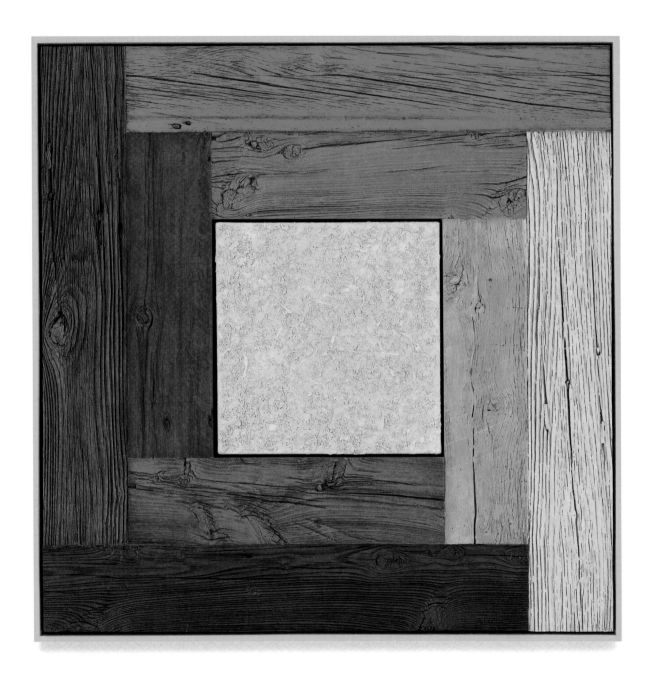

Left – right:

Untitled (SHRooMS), 2021
Watercolor and collage on paper with artist frame (reclaimed wood)
14 ⁵/₈ x 11 ³/₄ inches
37.1 x 29.8 cm

Left – right:

Untitled (SHRooMS), 2021
Watercolor and collage on paper with artist frame (reclaimed wood)
14 ⅝ x 11 ¾ inches
37.1 x 29.8 cm

DOUGLAS MELINI

Born in New Jersey in 1972
Lives and works in Jersey City, NJ

EDUCATION

1997
MFA, California Institute of the Arts, Valencia, CA

1994
BA, University of Maryland, College Park, MD

SOLO EXHIBITIONS

2021
Miles McEnery Gallery, New York, NY

2020
"Into The Woods," SOCO Gallery, Charlotte, NC

2018
"Starry Sky," Van Doren Waxter, New York, NY
"When the Moon Hangs on the Wall: Landscapes, Seascapes, and
    Abstracts," Schneider Museum of Art, Ashland, OR

2017
"Douglas Melini," Phillip Slein Gallery, St. Louis, MO
"You Have to Peer Into the Sky to See the Stars," 11R, New York, NY

2014
"Douglas Melini," Eleven Rivington, New York, NY

2012
"A Sharing of Color and Being Part of It," Feature Inc., New York, NY

2011
The Suburban, Oak Park, IL

2009
"It Flows Over Us Without Meaning," Minus Space, New York, NY

2005
"Beyond the Dirty Light," Ursula Werz, Tübingen, Germany

2004
"Positively Do Not Block the Gate," Rocket Gallery, London,
    United Kingdom

2003
"White Room," White Columns, New York, NY
"Head On," Homeroom, Munich, Germany

1999
Rocket Gallery, London, United Kingdom

1998
Richard Heller Gallery, Los Angeles, CA

1997
"MFA Thesis Show," Gallery D301, California Institute of the Arts,
    Valencia, CA

GROUP EXHIBITIONS

2020
"Energy in All Directions," The Frances Young Tang Teaching Museum
    and Art Gallery at Skidmore College, Saratoga Springs, NY

2019
"Chroma," Van Doren Waxter, New York, NY
"Pulled in Brooklyn" (curated by Roberta Waddell and Samantha
    Rippner), International Print Center New York, New York, NY
"The Twenty By Sixteen Biennial," Morgan Lehman, New York, NY

2018
"People, Place and Things...," Philip Slein Gallery, St Louis, MO
"Geometric Behavior," Ikast Kunstpakhuset, Copenhagen, Denmark

2017
"Edge," Philip Slein Gallery, St Louis, MO

2016
"Confluence/Influence in Contemporary Abstraction" (curated by
    Bridget Donlon and Leslie Wayne), Dorsky Gallery Curatorial
    Programs, New York, NY
11R, New York, NY

2015
"Eat a Peach," Jeff Bailey Gallery, Hudson, NY
"Breaking Pattern," Schneider Museum of Art, Ashland, OR
"Colour and Line," RaygunLab, Toowoomba, Australia
"Breaking Pattern," Minus Space Gallery, New York, NY

2014
"This One's Optimistic: Pincushion" (curated by Cary Smith),
    New Britain Museum of American Art, New Britain, CT
"Element of Style," Geoffrey Young Gallery, Great Barrington, MA

2013
"Decenter: An Exhibition on the Centenary of the 1913 Armory Show"
    (curated by Andrianna Campbell-LaFleur and Daniel S. Palmer),
    Abrons Art Center, New York, NY and Luther W. Brady Art Gallery,
    George Washington University, Washington, D. C.

2012
"Punt," Feature Inc., New York, NY
"X-Centric," Geoffrey Young Gallery, Great Barrington, MA
"Chromacosm," Fred Giampietro Gallery, New Haven, CT

2011
"Self Referral Nonobjective," Feature Inc., New York, NY
"Douglas Melini, Gary Peterson, Sarah Walker," McKenzie Fine Art,
    New York, NY
"Drawing Crazy Patterns on the Sheets," Geoffrey Young Gallery,
    Great Barrington, MA
"bodybraingame," Rhona Hoffman Gallery, Chicago, IL
"I Am Not Monogamous, I Heart Poetry," Feature Inc., New York, NY

"The Working Title" (organized by Progress Report), Bronx River Art
    Center, New York, NY
"Cries & Whispers" (curated by Paul W. Evans), Sam Lee Gallery,
    Los Angeles, CA
"Landing Jam" (curated by Martin Esteves), The Ugly Art Room,
    New York, NY

2010
"Strategic Abstraction," Geoffrey Young Gallery, Great Barrington, MA
"Power to the People," Feature Inc., New York, NY
"Anti-Anti/Non-Non" (curated by Fran Halstrom), Hal Bromm,
    New York, NY

2009
"Friends in High Places" (curated by Zach Needler and Adrian Ting),
    Christopher Henry Gallery, New York, NY

2008
"Me(n)tal" (curated by Dimitrios Antonitsis), Ileana Tounta
    Contemporary Art Center, Athens, Greece
"Minus Space: A Survey of Reductive and Post Minimal Work"
    (curated by Phong Bui), MoMA PS1, New York, NY

2007
"Machine Learning" (curated by Matthew Deleget), The Boyden
    Gallery, St. Mary's College of Maryland, St. Mary's City, MD, traveled
    to The Painting Center, New York, NY and Gallery Sonja Roesch,
    Houston, TX
"Men & Math" (curated by Maika Pollack), Southfirst Gallery,
    New York, NY

2006
"The Difficult Shapes of Possible Images" (organized by Douglas Melini),
    ZieherSmith Gallery, New York, NY

2005
"Mallorca Open: Principles of Construction" (curated by Friederike
    Nymphius), Kunsthalle del Centro Cultural Andratx, Mallorca, Spain

2004
"Minimalism and After III," DaimlerChrysler Contemporary, Berlin,
   Germany
"Benefit Exhibition," White Columns, New York, NY
"Open Range" (curated by Sima Familiant and Augusto Arbizo),
   Greenberg Van Doren Gallery, New York, NY

2003
"Two by Two for Aids and Art," Dallas Art Museum, Dallas, TX
"3-2-1" (curated by Cara Pearlman), Gallery M, New York, NY

2002
"Abstract Redux," Danese Gallery, New York, NY

1998
"LA Cool," Rocket Gallery, London, United Kingdom
Bruning and Ziscke Gallery, Düsseldorf, Germany

AWARDS AND GRANTS

2013
Marie Walsh Sharpe Foundation Studio Residency,
   Colorado Springs, CO

2008
New York Foundation for the Arts Fellowship in Painting, New York, NY

2007
Artist's Fellowship, Change Inc., New York, NY

SELECT COLLECTIONS

Daimler Collection, Berlin, Germany

Jill and Peter Kraus Collection, Dutchess County, NY

Frances Young Tang Teaching Museum and Art Gallery at Skidmore
   College, Saratoga Springs, NY

Neuberger Berman Art Collection, New York, NY

Progressive Corporation, Cleveland, OH

Wellspring Capital Corporation, New York, NY

Published on the occasion of the exhibition

DOUGLAS MELINI

9 September – 16 October 2021

Miles McEnery Gallery
511 West 22nd Street
New York NY 10011

tel +1 212 445 0051
www.milesmcenery.com

Publication © 2021 Miles McEnery Gallery
All rights reserved
Essay © 2021 Sara Roffino

Director of Publications
Anastasija Jevtovic, New York, NY

Photography by
Christopher Burke Studio, New York, NY

Color separations by
Echelon, Santa Monica, CA

Catalogue designed by
McCall Associates, New York, NY

ISBN: 978-1-949327-51-9

Cover: *Untitled (Tree Painting-Double L, Pink, Orange, and Blue)*, (detail), 2021

MILES
McENERY
GALLERY